SPEED RACERS

RACING DIRT BIKES

Jane Katirgis and
James Holter

Enslow Publishing
101 W. 23rd Street
Suite 240
New York, NY 10011
USA
enslow.com

Published in 2018 by Enslow Publishing, LLC.
101 W. 23rd Street, Suite 240, New York, NY 10011

Library of Congress Cataloging-in-Publication Data

Names: Katirgis, Jane, author. | Holter, James, author.
Title: Racing dirt bikes / Jane Katirgis and James Holter.
Description: New York : Enslow Publishing, [2018] | Series: Speed racers | Includes bibliographical references and index.
Identifiers: LCCN 2017021677| ISBN 9780766092754 (library bound) | ISBN 9780766094147 (pbk.) | ISBN 9780766094154 (6 pack)
Subjects: LCSH: Motorcycle racing—Juvenile literature. | Trail bikes—Juvenile literature.
Classification: LCC GV1060 . K37 2018 | DDC 796.7/5—dc23
LC record available at https://lccn.loc.gov/2017021677

Printed in the United States of America

To Our Readers: We have done our best to make sure all websites in this book were active and appropriate when we went to press. However, the author and the publisher have no control over and assume no liability for the material available on those websites or on any websites they may link to. Any comments or suggestions can be sent by email to customerservice@enslow.com.

Portions of this book originally appeared in the book *Dirt Bike Racers* by James Holter.

Photo Credits: Cover, p. 1 Edu Silva 2ev/Shutterstock.com; p. 4 Songdech Kothmongkol/Shutterstock.com; pp. 5, 7, 8, 11 Erick W. Rasco/Sports Illustrated/Getty Images; p. 9 Hyoung Chang/Denver Post/Getty Images; pp. 13, 19 Anatoliy Evankov/Shutterstock.com; p. 14 Lars Baron/Bongarts/Getty Images; p. 17 Allen J. Schaben/Los Angeles Times/Getty Images; pp. 21, 25 Vytautas Kielaitis/Shutterstock.com; p. 23 konmesa/Shutterstock.com; pp. 27, 34 Icon Sportswire/Getty Images; pp. 29, 37 StockStudio/Shutterstock.com; p. 32 Pedro Monteiro/Shutterstock.com; pp. 36, 41 Gines Romero/Shutterstock.com; p. 38 Christian Pondella/Getty Images.

Contents

1. Racing Off Road 4
2. Dirt Bike History 8
3. Dirt Bike Basics: The Bike 13
4. Time to Ride 21
5. Staying Safe 29
6. Racing Your Dirt Bike 36

Glossary 43

Further Reading 45

Index 47

Racing Off Road

1

It is opening day of the AMA Supercross Championships. Fans gather to cheer for their favorite riders. The racers are ready to speed over a dirt racetrack on their motorized dirt bikes. Jumping, turning, and spinning their wheels while whipping around corners, each rider will concentrate intently during the entire race. Who will finish victorious? Who will wipe out? Who will be the new face to watch as the season unfolds?

At the starting line of the 2017 AMA Supercross at MetLife Stadium in New Jersey, racers are ready for the competition.

The Race Begins

Forty racers are lined up side by side. They rev the engines on their dirt bikes. The riders lean over their handlebars and watch the metal starting gate. Their front wheels inch toward the gate with each blip of their throttles.

The gate drops! The racers fire off the line. Their front wheels lift off the ground as they battle for position down a long straightaway.

One rider enters the first turn ahead of the pack. His bike is sliding sideways, but he's in total control. As the leader completes the turn, he twists his throttle harder. He speeds over a large jump and leaps thirty feet (nine meters) down the track. The rest of the pack follows. Two, three, even four riders jump side by side. They all have the same goal: to win the motocross race.

Racing Off-Road Motorcycles

Motocross—also called MX—is a sport for racing off-road motorcycles. Riders complete several laps around a course of jumps, turns, hills, and bumps. The winner is the first to complete the assigned number of laps.

Personalize Your Ride

The look of your bike is up to you. You can buy graphics in many colors and sizes, and you can put them on your bike wherever you like. You might like the look of many graphics, or you might prefer just a couple for a cleaner look. You don't want your graphics to fade or crack, so purchase ones with protective coatings.

Star on the Track

Twenty-seven-year-old Ryan Dungey is a dominant racer in motocross. He has won every title in the sport. After turning pro in 2006, he became the second youngest rider to win both the Supercross and Motocross championships in his rookie year.

As you will read later in this book, racing is often a family affair. And that is true for Dungey. His father and two siblings were amateur dirt bike

Top racer Ryan Dungey takes a turn during the 2017 Monster Energy AMA Supercross.

riders, and they often travel with him during his racing season. Since 2012, Dungey has been a big part of the River-to-River Ride in Minnesota, with proceeds benefiting the St. Jude Children's Research Hospital. It is a way for him and many other riders to support families who rely on the hospital when they are struggling with childhood cancer and other life-threatening diseases.

Dirt Bike History

2

Today, motocross is a popular sport. The national championships draw huge crowds. The X Games are an exciting event every year, with the thrill of the race unfolding in front of many fans. How did this sport of speed, adventure, and adrenaline begin?

Motocross racing started in England in the 1920s. Road motorcyclists wanted to see who could ride fastest on tough off-road terrain. On early motocross tracks, the only obstacles were bumps and hills like the ones in any farmer's field. These natural-terrain obstacles seem tame now. Back then they were intense!

Motocross races take place on outdoor courses.

Today, motocross tracks look very different. They still include natural-terrain obstacles, but they also have man-made jumps. Today's professional racers can fly 100 ft (30 m) through the air off those jumps. Modern tracks also have whoop-de-dos, off-camber turns, and deep ruts.

Motocross and Supercross are the most popular dirt bike racing events. They do have similarities, and both races invite the top athletes to attend. There is jumping, tight turns, and, of course, dirt! So, what is the difference? It has to do with how the courses are made.

In the summer, pros race in the American Motorcyclist Association (AMA) National Motocross Championship. In the winter, they ride in the AMA Supercross Championship. Motocross races happen outdoors.

Supercross races are on man-made courses inside large stadiums. Supercross began in the 1970s. Since then, all the top riders have raced in both Motocross and Supercross.

AMA Motocross Championships

The AMA Motocross Championships are held every year between the middle of May and the end of August. The series started in 1972, and the women's championship began in 1996.

They event takes place over twelve rounds, each at a different major track in the United States. The championship has three classes. They are:

1. 250 cc class
2. 450 cc class
3. Women's class

The reigning 2016 champion in the 250 class is Cooper Webb, and Ken Roczen holds the 450 class title. The women's winner in 2016 was Kylie Fasnacht, who held on to her 2015 title by winning a second year in a row.

AMA Supercross Championships

The Supercross Championship series started in 1974. Every January, the Supercross begins and runs through the beginning of May. They are held in major league football and baseball stadiums. The classes for this series are:

1. 250 cc West (eight rounds)
2. 250 cc East (eight rounds)
3. 450 cc (seventeen rounds)

The 2017 champ in the 250 cc West class was Justin Hill. Zach Osborne won the 2017 250 cc East title. Ryan Dungey won the 450 cc in 2017 for a third year in a row.

Supercross races take place in stadiums across the country.

Motocross Fame

Famous dirt bike racers include Roger DeCoster from the 1960s, Bob Hannah from the 1970s, Rick Johnson and Jeff Ward from the 1980s, and Jeremy McGrath from the 1990s.

Retired racer Ricky Carmichael is considered the greatest motocross racer of all time. He has won the most national motocross championships in history. Today's top racers include Ryan Dungey, Justin Hill, Jeremy Martin, Marvin Musquin, and Cooper Webb.

Other Types of Dirt Bike Racing

Motocross is not the only type of dirt bike racing. Other races are held in the woods or on flat, oval tracks.

All types of dirt bike racing have a few things in common, though. First, the races happen on the dirt. Second, racers almost always ride on motocross bikes that they have changed to fit their type of racing. Third, the races are all great fun!

Hare Scrambles: A hare scramble is a race of several laps around a marked trail in the woods. Hare scrambles bikes often have hand guards, soft suspension, and bash plates. These plates protect the bottom of the engine from rocks.

Dirt Track: Dirt track is a race around an oval-shaped course. Racers go counterclockwise, so they make only left turns. Dirt track bikes have smoother tires and are often lowered to better handle high speeds on long straightaways.

TT Racing: TT racing is like dirt track. However, the course has at least one right turn and one jump.

Hillclimb: In hillclimb, riders see who can make it up a hill the fastest. If no one makes it to the top, the racer who gets the farthest wins. Hillclimb bikes often have longer swingarms, which are parts that support the rear wheel.

3 Dirt Bike Basics: The Bike

Many pro riders began riding on a Yamaha PW50 bike. Other popular beginner bikes are the KTM 50 SX Mini, the Cobra CX50 JR, and the Honda CRF50F. Of course, bikes are expensive, so start with a used model if you can. You want to be sure you enjoy the sport before you spend lots of money on a bike and accessories.

A beginner bike, or trail bike, is designed to be easy to ride. These motorcycles increase power more slowly than race bikes. Some beginner bikes have automatic clutches. They also have softer suspension. This means they travel more smoothly over small

Young riders start out riding on beginner bikes. They focus on basic skills and safety.

bumps. Even the best riders learn to ride on beginner bikes. These bikes let you focus on learning the proper skills.

Most beginner bikes are quiet. They come with exhausts that allow the bikes to be ridden on public trails. But beginner bikes are not built to handle big jumps, and they don't go as fast as race bikes. Do you want to go faster and jump farther? It's time to consider a race bike.

Find the Right Beginner Bike

There are many beginner bikes available today. These bikes feature automatic clutches:

- Honda CRF50 and CRF70
- Yamaha PW50, TTR50, and TTR110

- Suzuki DR-Z70
- Kawasaki KLX110
- KTM 50 SX Mini Adventure
- Cobra CX50 JR

These bikes have manual clutches but are still easy to ride:

- Honda CRF80 and CRF100
- Yamaha TTR-125
- Suzuki DR-Z125
- Kawasaki KLX140

Race Bikes

Race bikes are designed for quick acceleration and high top speed. Speed is the distance something travels in a set amount of time. Saying that a dirt bike goes forty miles (sixty-four kilometers) per hour describes its speed. Acceleration is the rate of change of speed. For example, a dirt bike that accelerates fast builds speed quickly. For tracks with lots of corners and big jumps, fast acceleration is important. For flatter tracks with long, straight sections, high top speed is important.

The suspension on race bikes can handle large jumps. Race bikes are designed to be much lighter than beginner bikes.

Gravity pulls you back to the ground when you jump into the air. Think how hard it would be to jump while holding a heavy dirt bike! To leap high, dirt bike racers have to go fast and ride over steep jumps.

Because they are built for high performance, race bikes cost more money than beginner bikes. They also need more maintenance.

Race bikes are designed for closed-course tracks. They are not allowed on trails. They are too loud, and small sparks from their exhausts could start a fire.

Some smaller race bikes have automatic clutches. They should not be mistaken for beginner bikes, though. These race bikes are still very fast and unsafe for beginners. These race bikes have automatic clutches:

- KTM 50 SX
- Cobra CX50
- Polini X1R and X3R

These race bikes have manual clutches:

- Kawasaki KX65 and KX85
- KTM 65 SX, 85 SX, and 105 SX
- Suzuki RM85
- Yamaha YZ85
- Honda CR85 and CRF150R

Manual or Automatic?

You might be wondering what the difference is between automatic and manual clutches. An automatic clutch does not require the rider to shift gears and operate a clutch. It happens automatically. An automatic clutch allows a rider to work on the basic skills of riding and staying upright before mastering the more detailed skill of operating a clutch.

The suspension on a race bike can handle large jumps. Here, Ricky Carmichael makes a jump during a Supercross competition in rain and thick mud.

Tips for Choosing a Bike

Motosport.com lists some guidelines for choosing the right dirt bike. They include:

1. Don't go big! Start with a small 50 cc engine and small bike size.
2. Try to get a used bike to help you save money. Members of a local dirt bike community or club may be selling their starter bikes or know people who can sell a used bike to you. Buy a name brand used bike, which comes with the reliability and toughness that a quality-company product provides.
3. Make sure the bike fits you. If the bike is too large, it will be hard to handle. Your feet should sit evenly on the ground when you are seated, and you should be able to reach the handlebars and controls easily.
4. Take the bike for a test, whether it is used or new. If a 50 cc bike is too small, consider looking at a bike with a 70 or 80 cc engine.
5. Starter bikes for kids can sometimes advertise add-on features, such as automatic liquid-cooled transmissions. Just remember, the more extras you add, the more money you will spend.

A Fine-Tuned Bike

If you don't keep your motorcycle in good shape, it will not perform at the top of its game. You have to learn how to maintain your dirt bike.

The most important tool for taking care of your bike is the manufacturer's service manual. The service manual tells you how to keep your machine running strong.

Some maintenance jobs require special tools and knowledge. For these jobs, take your motorcycle to your local dealership.

Working on your motorcycle isn't just about maintenance. There are many products that you can add to your dirt bike to make it cooler.

Make sure you maintain your bike properly so that it performs its best during every jump and every ride.

Most dirt bike racers buy special sticker kits for their bikes. Some buy brightly colored plastic fenders.

Modern motorcycles have different suspension, engine, and control settings. This means you can set up your bike just the way you like it without spending more money. Make sure you ask an adult for help whenever you work on your motorcycle.

4 Time to Ride

Some people like to start riding when they are as young as possible. Maybe they are only four or five years old. Some racing experts say that a young age is a perfect time to start dirt bike riding. As riders get older, they get more fearful. Better to start before you get too nervous! It is also cheaper to start young; this way, if the sport is not for you, you can move on to something else before you invest years of time and money.

Basic Training

Learning to ride a motorcycle can be fun. The key is to have a good attitude. Don't ride too fast. Also, stay away from terrain that is too difficult for you or your motorcycle.

Before you can go fast or take big jumps, you need to learn the basics. A motocross bike is powered by a gasoline engine. A twist throttle on the right handgrip controls the power of the engine. A clutch lever near the left handgrip controls how much of that power passes to the transmission. The front brake lever is near the right handgrip. The rear brake lever is near the right footpeg.

One of the hardest controls to learn is the clutch. To practice, release the clutch slowly while turning the throttle slightly. When the motorcycle starts to edge forward, gently squeeze the clutch back in, close the throttle, and repeat.

Laws of Motion and Brakes

Have you heard of the scientist Isaac Newton? Newton's first law of motion states that a body in motion will stay in motion until a force acts on it to change its motion. This applies to a dirt bike, too: a dirt bike in motion will tend to stay in motion. That's why the brakes are just as important as the throttle. Sometimes you will have to squeeze the brakes hard to slow down enough to turn at a corner.

The First Steps to Speed

Riding a motorcycle quickly and safely takes practice. Let's start with the basics.

To get a good start, watch the starting gate closely. Gently let out your clutch until your motorcycle barely nudges forward as you turn the throttle. When the gate drops, turn the throttle quickly—but not so fast that your front wheel lifts too high off the ground.

If you start riding when you are young, you will not be as nervous to try the new sport.

The most important riding skill is cornering. When you corner, you must be smooth with your throttle. If you turn your throttle too quickly, your rear tire will spin. As you go through the corner, lean your motorcycle in the direction you are turning.

Hills are a common MX obstacle. Traction is different when you are going uphill. You need to lean forward to keep from flipping over backward. If you lean forward too far, your rear wheel can spin.

Motocross tracks develop a lot of ruts. Most ruts form in the corners. When you ride through a rut, stay smooth and steady. If you make any sudden shifts in direction, you can fall over.

Mastering the Corner

Dirt bike riders often stick out their inside legs when they go around a corner. This riding position actually helps with balance as they lean the bike over. Another trick is to press down on the outside footpeg. This gives you better traction.

Riding Tracks

Motocross tracks are not as common as baseball fields or basketball courts. Luckily, it can be easy to find a place to ride if you know where to look. Start by talking to people who work at a motorcycle dealership near your home. They can tell you about local tracks.

You also can find tracks by searching online. Ask your parents to help you look up local tracks and riding areas. Then give the tracks a call. Find out when they are open and how much they charge to ride.

Some tracks are sandy, while others have hard-packed dirt. Some tracks have big hills. Some are built in flat fields.

You will use your brakes to slow down around a corner. Notice that a rider often sticks out his or her inside leg when going around a corner.

Some tracks have special times for smaller motorcycles and young riders to be on the track. If you ride a smaller dirt bike, it's dangerous to share the track with full-size motorcycles.

Some track owners take time to prepare their tracks during the day. They water the track to keep down the dust. Then the staff uses heavy machinery to smooth out the track's surface.

Find the Right Balance

Today's motocross tracks are filled with tough obstacles. If you want to win the race, you have to ride over these obstacles safely and quickly.

The fastest way over an obstacle is not always the safest. However, the safest way is not always the fastest! The best riders find a balance between safety and speed. This helps them get ahead of the pack and stay there.

Finding that balance takes a lot of practice. That's why you should always start slowly and then build up to trying difficult terrain. Practice each type of obstacle many times before you move on to the next one. This is a good way to gain confidence.

Jumping Tips

Some whoop-de-dos are small. Other whoop-de-dos are as large as small jumps. The most important thing is to hit them straight. If you hit them at an angle, it will be hard to keep a steady speed.

When you hit a jump, stand up and lean forward slightly. Be steady with the throttle. If you turn your throttle too hard, you can flip over backward. If you cut your throttle before you jump off the top, you can flip forward.

There are different types of jumps. On a single jump, you land on flat ground. On a double jump, you land on the backside of a second jump.

Racer Paul Coates stands up and leans forward at the lip of a Supercross triple jump.

A tabletop is like a double jump, but the space between the two jumps is filled in with dirt.

Riding Schools

Do you want to go faster on your dirt bike? Don't spend a lot of money to make your motorcycle faster. Instead, go to a riding school to make yourself go faster. Expert racers will teach you how to corner and jump the proper way. They will talk about the right attitude and training habits for racing.

Most riding schools are well organized. The trainers have been riding for many years, and they know the best ways to go fast on a motocross track. You can learn a lot from videos and books, but the best advice comes from one-on-one instruction.

There are riding schools for all experience levels. Beginner schools teach you the basics. Advanced schools cover more difficult techniques.

Professional trainers sell books and videos that demonstrate the best riding methods. Gary Semics has been training both new and experienced riders since 1985. He has produced many books and videos on his techniques.

5 Staying Safe

It is not a pleasant thought, but injuries and crashing happen. They are a part of the sport. Dirt bike riders never intend to crash, but they all take a spill or two. Safety gear protects you when you crash. Even slow crashes hurt!

Although wiping out is unnerving, it is important not to be afraid to later get back on the bike. Wear the proper riding equipment, because without safety gear, you are more likely to get seriously hurt in a motocross race.

Almost all track owners require safety equipment. Even if you only ride in your own backyard, you should always protect yourself.

Helmet for Safety

The most important piece of safety gear is a helmet. A helmet must fit snugly on your head. A loose helmet will slide around as you ride. It won't protect your head if you crash.

Some things to consider when buying your helmet include:

1. Safety first! Check out the minimum safety standards set by the US Department of Transportation (DOT) for helmet protection.
2. Are helmets different for boys and girls? No, bike helmets are the same for girls and boys. The important thing is the correct fit.
3. Are you a beginner or seasoned rider? If you are a beginner rider, don't break the bank with the most expensive helmet. Don't skimp on safety, but be sure you will continue in the sport before you go over budget. Once you are ready for an upgrade or replacement, you can think more about what features you want in your helmet.
4. What is the helmet weight? Does it have air vents? Remember that a heavy helmet adds to a claustrophobic, closed-in feeling. Air vents help the helmet feel more open.
5. What is the helmet made of? Most kid helmets are polycarbonate, poly alloy, or polycarbonate blends. These materials offer safety and strength, but they are not as expensive as fiberglass and carbon fiber. A removable, washable liner can be cleaned. Other liners have antimicrobial materials to minimize unwanted bacterial growth.

More Protection

You'll need protective eye goggles, boots, kneepads, and gloves. Most riders also wear elbow pads, riding pants, a riding jersey, a chest protector, and a neck brace. A chest protector provides extra padding around your chest and back. Some chest protectors are large plastic guards that fit over your jersey. Others are small, light foam pads that you wear next to your skin.

Buy your first set of safety gear from a local motorcycle dealer rather than ordering it online or by mail. That way, you can try the gear on to make sure it fits comfortably. The dealer also can answer questions about different brands and types of gear.

Sizing Tips for Your Helmet

Measure your head by having a friend or parent wrap a measuring tape around your head, half an inch above your ears, eyebrows, and the widest point of the back of your head. Match this measurement to the specs shown for different helmet sizes. Each brand will have different sizing. Then try the helmet on for size and comfort. It should not be too loose or too tight. Be sure that it feels snug on your head but you can speak easily without biting your cheeks. And although you will be growing, don't buy a larger helmet that you will "grow into." To work properly, a helmet has to fit you snugly and securely *now*.

Stay Within Your Limits

Athletes can get hurt playing any sport. Motocross is no different. Riding a motorcycle fast over jumps, hills, and bumps is fun. It also can be dangerous if you aren't careful.

The rider is most responsible for his or her own safety. It is important to know how fast you can ride safely and to ride within those limits. If you ride within your limits, chances are you will not crash.

Know the limits of your motorcycle. Do not ride in places where it cannot go. Do not ride it faster than it should go. And remember that not all terrain is safe for riding. Be very careful in areas with cliffs, rocks, loose riding surfaces such as gravel, and steep hillsides.

Always make sure your helmet fits properly, and wear it during every ride.

When riding, do NOT use your dirt bike in these irresponsible ways:

- Riding off the proper track or trail
- Riding on trails without a spark arrestor
- Riding a loud racing bike anywhere but on a closed-course track
- Making ruts with your bike by spinning the rear tire on purpose

Collisions and Crashes

Some of the worst crashes happen when MX riders collide. You should always keep a safe distance from other riders. When you are racing, be careful as you pass other riders. If you are being passed, do not make any sudden moves that might cause a crash.

Everybody crashes sooner or later. Just follow these two tips, and you'll be fine. First, prepare for the worst by using safety gear. Second, when a crash does happen, learn from it.

Noah, a kid racer from Ohio, had been riding and racing for many years. He and his dad went to a practice day at a new track. His first time around the track, Noah crashed on a jump. He was going too fast when he hit it.

"I did not learn the new track before I tried to go fast," Noah said. "I should have ridden the track slowly first so I would know what to expect when I hit the jump going fast."

All motocross tracks are different. It is very important to ride them slowly. Then you will know how they are laid out before you speed up.

Elliot, also from Ohio, was new to dirt bike racing. He went to a race with his brother and dad. In his second race of the day, Elliot crashed in the whoop-de-dos. He wasn't hurt, but he broke the brake lever on his XR70.

"I was not going straight when I hit the whoop-de-dos," Elliot said. "I was riding at an angle when I hit the first bump, and I lost control of my motorcycle."

Crashes are part of the sport, and all riders eventually take a spill.

To stay safe on the track, riders need to look ahead. You can't prepare for an obstacle if you don't know it's coming.

Keep Earth Safe, Too

Dirt bike tracks and trails are almost always outside. Most of them are built in the country or in the woods. If you ride your dirt bike responsibly, you will not harm nature. If you are irresponsible, however, you can damage the planet.

Responsible riding protects the future of dirt bike racing. If riders damage the environment, they might not be allowed to use public land. Even private tracks might be closed down.

Few sports give kids as much freedom and control as dirt bike riding. And racing is as extreme and exciting as a sport can get. The choices you make as a dirt bike rider can play a big role in protecting the future of the sport.

Several organizations encourage responsible dirt bike riding. These include the American Motorcyclist Association, the BlueRibbon Coalition, the National Off-Highway Vehicle Conservation Council, and Americans for Responsible Recreational Access.

Racing Your Dirt Bike

6

After learning how to ride a dirt bike safely, many kids decide to race. Racing is fun and exciting. It tests your speed and skills against other riders. Motocross races are organized by adults. Races have rules to keep riders fair and safe.

It is a good idea to race at tracks where you have practiced. Then you will be familiar with the track. When you race, your body and your motorcycle have to be prepared. Racing is tough—but with dedication, practice, and patience, anyone can become an MX racer.

It is best to make your first race on a course that you are familiar with.

Finding a Race

AMA motocross races are listed on the AMA website. They are also published in the AMA magazine, which is mailed to members every month.

The top kid racers in the country face off every summer at the AMA Amateur Motocross Nationals in Hurricane Mills, Tennessee. Riders have to qualify to go to this race.

Race Day!

The race day scene at a motocross track is fast paced and exciting. The pits are packed with riders on all sizes of bikes. They are hustling

A Strong Young Woman

One of the sport's finest racers was Ashley Fiolek. Now retired and twenty-six years old, Fiolek was a member of the American Honda Red Bull Racing factory team. She raced in the Women's Motocross Association National Championship Series. At these events, she competed against the country's fastest female motocross racers.

Ashley Fiolek celebrates her gold medal at the Summer X Games in July 2010.

How good was Fiolek? She was the 2008, 2009, and 2011 WMX Motocross champion. She won the title in her first year as a pro! She won gold at the X Games, too, in 2009 and 2010. Fiolek was successful as an amateur racer, before she went pro, winning thirteen amateur national titles and more than one hundred races.

Here is another amazing fact about Fiolek: she is deaf. That doesn't slow her down, though. Fiolek overcame her challenges by training hard and staying focused. She was the first deaf person to appear on the late night show *Conan*. Today, she works as a motorcycle stuntwoman for a traveling show that features Marvel Comics characters. That is one adventurous life so far!

to get to the starting line or coming off the track, exhausted from their last race.

A lot happens on race days. All the events are well organized. For example, you are only allowed on the track at certain times. The track is well prepared. The dirt is watered to keep dust down, and the track crew smooths out ruts between races.

There are often additional safety rules on race day. For example, signs tell you where and when you're allowed to ride your dirt bike. Make sure you follow these rules, or you might be asked to leave the track.

Advertising at the Race

You will notice a lot of new signs on race day. Companies pay the track owner to put up their signs. This advertises their services and products to the racers and fans.

Follow the Racing Rules

Most American racetracks use rules that are written by the AMA. This is helpful when you travel to different tracks. Wherever you race, you will follow the same rules.

The rules of dirt bike racing cover these areas:

- The sizes of bikes that are allowed to race each other
- The ages of riders who are allowed to race each other
- The skill level of riders who are allowed to race each other
- How riders are allowed to modify their bikes to make them faster
- How riders advance to higher skill levels
- Safety guidelines for track owners

Outlaw Races

"Outlaw" races are races that are not run using AMA rules. These races are not really illegal. The term dates back to before the AMA started organizing races. At that time, many races were held on public streets. Those races really were against the law.

What to Expect on Race Day

On race day, you will be eager to get right on the track. You'll have to take a few first steps before you're set to ride.

As soon as you get to the track, you will go to the sign-up booth. Here you will choose your classes and pay your entry fee. There is usually a long line, so try to arrive early. You might even be able to sign up online before race day.

Shortly after sign-up closes, there will be a riders' meeting. Race officials will give you your practice group and race order. Then it will be time to hit the track for practice. Pay close attention to how the track has changed since you last rode there. Also, try taking the obstacles in different ways to find the fastest line.

The most common structure for a motocross race is a two-moto format. In a two-moto format, each class has two races. Each rider's combined score from the two motos determines his or her overall score. After all classes have raced both motos, trophies are awarded.

A Day for the Family

Race days are packed with tons of action off the track. Vendors sell everything from T-shirts to dirt bike parts. Fans line the fences to cheer on their friends and favorite riders.

Lots of kids go to dirt bike races, even if they don't race. They might be the brothers and sisters of the kids who do race. They come to watch, to hang out, and to cheer on their friends and family members.

Race day is exciting for all the racers and their family and friends.

Racing is a team effort. It's hard for a racer to win without strong support. Parents and siblings work on the bike, keep the gears and parts organized, and cheer loudly from the stands.

In some families, though, everyone races. A brother and sister might compete against each other on the track. Then they run back to the sidelines to cheer on mom or dad.

Support System

There will be times when the challenges of racing catch up to you. There will be broken parts on your motorcycle, banged-up parts on your body, and disappointing losses. It is much easier to overcome all of these challenges with the help and support of your family and friends.

Most families that race also go on trail rides. This is a great way for family members of all ages and skill levels to spend time together. Watching each other race is great, but riding together can be even better.

Some families stick together even after riders advance to the professional ranks. Jeremy and Alex Martin grew up riding as a team. Now they compete against each other as pro motocrossers. In July 2016, they shared the podium after placing first and third, respectively, in a pro Motocross 250 Class race at Spring Creek MX Park in Millville, Minnesota.

Glossary

acceleration The rate at which an object's speed increases.

American Motorcyclist Association (AMA) An organization that oversees street and off-road motorcycling and protects the rights of motorcyclists. It also makes rules for most amateur motorcycle racing in the United States.

bash plates Thick metal plates that protect a motorcycle engine from rocks.

closed-course tracks Tracks that are restricted to a specified area, usually away from woods and neighborhoods.

clutch A part that controls how much energy from the engine passes to the transmission. When the clutch is fully engaged, all the engine's energy passes to the transmission. When the clutch is disengaged, no energy passes to the transmission. When the clutch is partially engaged, only some of the engine's energy passes to the transmission.

cornering Riding a dirt bike around a turn on a racetrack.

exhausts Pipes that carry fumes from a motorcycle's engine into the air.

natural-terrain obstacles Obstacles that result from natural changes in the earth, such as hills, drop-offs, and dips.

neck brace A device that fits between a helmet and a person's shoulders. It keeps your neck from bending too far in any direction if you crash.

off-camber turns Turns where the ground slopes in the opposite direction of the turn. For example, in a left-hand turn, the ground would slope toward the right.

pits Areas around a racetrack where riders park and wait for a race to start.

race classes Groups of racers organized by age, experience, and/or motorcycle size. Each class is scored separately.

ruts Ditches created in the dirt by dirt bike tires.

spark arrestor A part of a motorcycle's exhaust that prevents sparks from coming out.

straightaway A section of a track that doesn't have any turns.

suspension The parts of a dirt bike that soak up bumps and landings from big jumps.

swingarms Straight pieces of steel or aluminum that connect the rear wheel to the rest of a motorcycle.

throttles Devices that control the speed of a motorcycle.

traction The ability to grip a surface.

transmission The gears inside a motorcycle that determine how much of the engine's energy it takes to turn the rear wheel. You shift through the gears using a small lever by your left foot. In lower gears, the motorcycle accelerates quickly but has a low top speed. In higher gears, the motorcycle accelerates slowly but has a high top speed. The rider shifts gears to maintain the best acceleration and speed for the terrain.

whoop-de-dos Series of bumps on a motocross track.

Further Reading

Books

Adamson, Thomas K. *Motocross Freestyle*. Minneapolis, MN: Bellwether Media, Inc., 2016.

Adamson, Thomas K. *Motocross Racing*. Minneapolis, MN: Bellwether Media, Inc., 2016.

Castellano, Peter. *Motocross*. New York, NY: Gareth Stevens Publishing, 2016.

Koll, Hilary. *A Math Journey Through Extreme Sports*. New York, NY: Crabtree Publishing Co., 2016.

Maddox, Jake. *Motocross*. North Mankato, MN: Stone Arch Books, 2016.

Websites

AMERICAN MOTORCYCLIST ASSOCIATION

americanmotorcyclist.com

The official website of the American Motorcyclist Association

MX SPORTS

mxsports.com

News about the qualifiers and championship races for the AMA Amateur Motocross Nationals

OFF-ROAD.COM

off-road.com

Bike reviews and tips for racing your dirt bike

WOMEN'S MOTOCROSS ASSOCIATION (WMA)

womensmotocrossassociation.com

Read about ladies-only events, stars, and race results

Index

A

age, 21, 26, 39, 42
AMA Motocross Championship, 6, 10
AMA Supercross Championship, 4, 6, 9, 10
Amateur Motocross Nationals, 37
American Motorcyclist Association (AMA), 9, 10, 35, 37, 39
Americans for Responsible Recreational Access, 35

B

beginners, 13–14, 15, 18, 30
BlueRibbon Coalition, 35

C

Carmichael, Ricky, 12
clutches, 13, 14, 15, 16, 22
collisions, 33
cornering, 24
cost, 15, 17, 28
crashes, 33

D

DeCoster, Roger, 12
dirt tracks, 12, 24, 39
Dungey, Ryan, 6–7, 10, 12

F

Fasnacht, Kylie, 10
Fiolek, Ashley, 38

G

gear, 30–31

H

Hannah, Bob, 12
hare scramble, 12
helmet, 30, 31
Hill, Justin, 10, 12
hillclimb, 12
history, 8, 10

J

Johnson, Rick, 12
jumps, 6, 9, 15, 26, 28

L

limits, 31

M

maintenance, 15, 18
Martin, Jeremy, 12
McGrath, Jeremy, 12
motocross (MX), 6, 8, 9, 11, 24, 26, 31, 40
Musquin, Marvin, 12

N

National Off-Highway Vehicle Conservation Council, 35

O

obstacles, 8, 9, 24, 26, 40
off road, 6, 12, 35
Osborne, Zach, 10
outlaw races, 40

P

personalization, 6, 20
philanthropy, 7
professionals, 6–7, 9, 10, 12, 13, 42

R

race bikes, 15, 16, 37
racing, 5, 6, 8, 9, 10, 12, 28, 29, 33, 35, 36, 37, 39, 41
racing types, 12
River-to-River Ride, 7
Roczen, Ken, 10

S

safety, 26, 29, 30, 31, 39
skills, 24, 26, 28
speed, 8, 12, 15, 22, 24, 31, 33
suspension, 12, 13, 15, 20

T

throttle, 22, 24, 26
tips, 16
tracks, 9, 12, 24, 26, 33, 35, 39, 40
traction, 24
training, 22, 28
TT racing, 12

W

Ward, Jeff, 12
Webb, Cooper, 10, 12
whoop-de-dos, 9, 26, 33
women, 10, 38
Women's Motocross Association (WMA) National Championship, 38

X

X Games, 8